Latin
Shortcut

By

Irenaeus De Oliveira Iunior

Copyright © 2014 Irineu De Oliveira Jnr
All rights reserved.
ISBN:
ISBN-13: 978-1495337109
ISBN-10: 1495337103

INTRODUCTION. LINGUA LATINA	5
CAPITULUM I. PHONETIC LATIN ALPHABET	7
CAPITULUM II. THE LINGUISTIC SECRET	8
CAPITULUM III. ALIS	12
CAPITULUM IV. SIO	15
CAPITULUM V. TAS	17
CAPITULUM VI. TOR	20
CAPITULUM VII. ICUS	21
CAPITULUM VIII. ANTEM	25
CAPITULUM XIX. ENTEM	27
CAPITULUM X. ARE	29
CAPITULUM XI. ARIUS	32
CAPITULUM XII. MEMTUM	34
CAPITULUM XIII. ENTIA	36
CAPITULUM XIV. BILIS	38
CAPITULUM XV. IVUS	40
CAPITULUM XVI. FICARE	42
CAPITULUM XVII. GIA	44
CAPITULUM XVIII. ORIUS	46
CAPITULUM XIX. IDUS	48
CAPITULUM XX. IZARE	49
CAPITULUM XXI. ANTIA	51
CAPITULUM XXII. OSUS	53

CAPITULUM XXIII. SIS	55
CAPITULUM XXIV. ISMUS	57
CAPITULUM XXV. GRAMMA	59
CAPITULUM XXVI. EMA	61
CAPITULUM XXVII. UM	63
CAPITULUM XXVIII. URA	64
CAPITULUM XXIX. TUDO	66
CAPITULUM XXX. TIA	68
CAPITULUM XXXI. PHIA	70
CAPITULUM XXXII. ESSUS	72
CAPITULUM XXXIII. GUS	73
CAPITULUM XXXIV. EA	74
CAPITULUM XXXV. CULUM	75
CAPITULUM XXXVI. US	77
CAPITULUM XXXVII. IA	79
CAPITULUM XXXVIII. PLUM OR PLUS	80
CAPITULUM XXXIX. ARIS	81
CAPITULUM XL. TRUM	83
CAPITULUM XLI. ETUM	85
CAPITULUM XLII. ENSUS	86
CAPITULUM XLIII. NUMERI ROMANI	87

INTRODUCTION.
Lingua Latina

Latin is often considered a 'dead language' in that it is no longer spoken as a native tongue by any group or culture at this particular time in history. However, it remains the language of science, and the root of many other languages.

At a point in history, it was arguably the most important language in the world, as it took its place as the lingua franca of the western world. It was a language shaped by culture and spread by conquest, it had a profound influence on the world then and that influence is still felt today.

Studying Latin is not just for classicists who wish to know more about the world of classical antiquity. Studying language is important to understand and grasp the basics of the Romance Languages which spring from Latin roots. In the twenty-first century, Latin terminology continues to influence medicine, law, and religion. Latin is still used in the form of inscriptions, medical taxonomy, legal jargon and religious ceremonies. In some countries of Central Europe it was in official use as recently as the first decades of the 19th century as the language of research and philosophy.

A brief history of Latin is useful to know. Latin is a member of the Indo-European Language family. It is descended from the Italic branch and is considered to be one of the oldest branches of Indo-European after Greek and Sanskrit.

The Italic branch broke off into two main branches: the Osco-Umbrian branch and the Latino-Falisco branch. These branches in turn yielded the Oscan and Umbrian Languages; and the Latin and Faliscan languages. From these branches, Latin experienced changes of development from its archaic form into a classical form, and later through medieval times, into various Romance languages.

The full history of the Latin language is diverse. The Romance languages which descend to us today are proof of its legacy. Latin's importance on the history of language development can never be underestimated.

CAPITULUM I.
Phonetic Latin Alphabet

Here is the alphabet phonetically written to allow you to compare the pronunciation of the English alphabet with the Latin alphabet.

So concentrate on practicing the pronunciation of those letters which are not familiar to you.

a ah **b** beh **c** keh **d** deh **e** ay **f** ehf

g gayh **h** hah **i** ee **j** iota **k** kah **l** ehl

m ehme **n** ehne **o** ohr **p** peh **q** coo

r eh-re **s** èhs **t** têh **u** oo **v** weh

w dooghpliu **x** eeks **y** ipsilon **z** zeyhta

Latin Shortcut

CAPITULUM II.
The Linguistic Secret

The linguistic secret is a conversion technique to identify Latin Words used in the English language.

For example, words ending in **TION** in English become **TIO** in Latin.

English	**LATINA**
Informa**tion**	Informa**tio**

Translate these words into Latin and then check the answers on the next page.

1. action _____
2. attention _____
3. confirmation _____
4. collection _____
5. communication _____
6. construction _____
7. contribution _____
8. question _____
9. education _____
10. imagination _____
11. option _____
12. transformation _____

Latin Shortcut

Here are the Latin words. Check if you got them right. You will also find many more words that you didn't know that you knew.

abbreviatio	coalitio	convictio
accumulatio	cognitio	cooperatio
accusatio	collaboratio	coordinatio
actio	collectio	corporatio
additio	commendatio	correctio
administratio	communicatio	correlatio
admiratio	compensatio	corruptio
adoptio	complicatio	creatio
adoratio	conceptio	declaratio
adulatio	conditio	decoratio
aemulatio	confederatio	definitio
aestimatio	confirmatio	demigratio
affiliatio	congregatio	demolitio
agitatio	conservatio	demonstratio
ambitio	consideratio	descriptio
animatio	consolatio	designatio
annotatio	consolidatio	destructio
anticipatio	constipatio	detentio
applicatio	constructio	dictrictio
assimilatio	contaminatio	directio
attentio	contemplatio	discretio
attenuatio	contractio	discriptio
attractio,	contradictio	dissertatio
auditio	contributio	distinctio
celebratio	contristatio	distributio
circulatio	conventio	dominatio

Latin Shortcut

editio	functio	intersectio,
educatio	germinatio	interventio
electio	gravitatio	introductio
electrocutio	identificatio	intuitio
elevatio	illustratio	inventio
eliminatio	imaginatio	invitatio
emancipatio	imitatio	irrigatio
erectio	imperfectio	irritatio
eruptio	improvisatio	iustificatio
evaporatio	inauguratio	legislatio
evolutio	incitatio	liberatio
excavatio	incorporatio	limitatio
exceptio	indiscretio	lotio
exclamatio	infectio	lubricatio
expeditio	inflammatio	malnutritio
exploratio	inflatio	manifestatio
expositio	informatio	meditatio
exstinctio	inhibitio	migratio
extraction	innovatio	moderatio
falsificatio	inquisitio	modificatio
fecundatio	inspiratio	multiplicatio
fermentatio	institutio	narratio
fictio	instructio	natio
fluctuatio	intentio	negotiatio
foederatio	interceptio	nominatio
fractio	interdicto,	notio
frictio	interpunctio	nutritio
fumigatio	interruptio	objectio

Latin Shortcut

obligatio	prostitutio	sedatio
observatio	protectio	seductio
obstructio	purificatio	segregatio
occupatio	quaestio	selectio
operatio	reactio	separatio
oppositio	receptio	simplicio
optio	reconciliatio	simulatio
ordinatio	recreatio	situatio
participatio	recuperatio	solutio
perceptio	reductio	specializacio
perfectio	reelectio	speculatio
persecutio	refrigeratio	stabilizatio
pertractatio	rehabilitatio	substructio
pollutio	renovatio	superstitio
portio	repetitio	traditio
praecautio	repraesentatio	transactio
praedictio	reputatio	transformatio
praemonitio	reservatio	transitio
praepositio	resolutio	transmigratio
praescriptio	respiratio	validatio
praesumptio	revelatio	variatio
productio	revolutio	vastatio
promotio	rotatio	ventilatio
promulgatio	satisfactio	vibratio
pronuntiatio	sectio	

Latin Shortcut

CAPITULUM III.
ALIS

Words ending in **AL** in English become **ALIS** in Latin.

Translate these words into Latin and then check the answers on the next page.

1. annual _____
2. central _____
3. cereal _____
4. special _____
5. Federal _____
6. initial _____
7. original _____
8. social _____
9. universal _____
10. total _____
11. vital _____
12. visual _____

Latin Shortcut

Here are the Latin words. Check if you got them right. You will also find many more words that you didn't know that you knew.

accidentalis	essentialis	integralis
antisocialis	experimentalis	intellectualis
annualis	fatalis	intentionalis
artificialis	foederalis	irrationalis
brutalis	festivalis	jovialis
canibalis	feudalis	lateralis
cathedralis	finalis	liberalis
caelestis	fiscalis	litteralis
centralis	formalis	localis
cerealis	fraternalis	manualis
caeremonialis	frugalis	martialis
conceptualis	fundamentalis	marginalis
conditionalis	grammaticalis	matrimonialis
constitutionalis	habitualis	materialis
conventionalis	horizontalis	menstrualis
corporalis	hospitalis	mentalis
criminalis	idealis	mineralis
decimalis	illegalis	modalis
diagonalis	impcrialis	monumentalis
dictatorius	impersonalis	moralis
differentialis	inauguralis	mortalis
essentialis	infernalis	universalis
specialis	initialis	municipalis
spinalis	immaterialis	muralis
spiritualis	immortalis	musicalis
exceptis	instrumentalis	nasalis

Latin Shortcut

naturalis	potentialis	supernaturalis
navalis	praesidentiale	socialis
nominalis	primordialis	superficialis
normalis	principalis	substantialis
officialis	proportionalis	terminalis
oralis	proverbialis	territorialis
ordinalis	provincialis	tonalis
originalis	punctualis	totalis
ovalis	rationalis	tradicionalis
papalis	radialis	transexualis
partialis	radicalis	unilateralis
parochialis	realis	usualis
pastoralis	ritualis	verbalis
pectoralis	rivalis	verticalis
pedalis	ruralis	virtualis
poenalis	carnalis	visualis
personalis	sensualis	vitalis
pluralis	sexualis	vocalis

Latin Shortcut

CAPITULUM IV.
SIO

words ending in **SION** in English become **SIO** in Latin.

Translate these words into Latin and then check the answers on the next page.

1. decision _____
2. division _____
3. emission _____
4. immersion _____
5. inclusion _____
6. mission _____
7. oppression _____
8. profession _____
9. correction _____
10. session _____
11. television _____
12. transmission _____

Latin Shortcut

Here are the Latin words. Check if you got them right. You will also find many more words that you didn't know that you knew.

abrasio	excursio	praetensio
admissio	expansio	processio
aggressio	explosio	professio
apprehensio	expressio	progressio
aversio	expulsio	propulsio
collisio	extensio	provisio
commissio	illusio	recessio
compassio	immersio	regressio
comprehensio	impressio	remissio
compressio	inclusio	repercussio
concessio	indecisio	repressio
conclusio	infusio	repulsio
confessio	intrusio	reversio
confusio	invasio	revisio
conversio	inversio	sessio
corrosio	mansio	subdivisio
decisio	missio	supervisio
decompressio	obsessio	suppressio
depressio	occasio	suspensio
diffusio	omissio	televisio
dimensio	oppressio	tensio
divisio	passio	transfusio
emissio	pensio	transgressio
emulsio	percussio	transmissio
erosio	persuasio	versio
exclusio	praecisio	visio

Latin Shortcut

CAPITULUM V.
TAS

Words ending in **TY** in English become **TAS** in Latin.

Translate these words into Latin and then check the answers on the next page.

1. anxiety   _____
2. authority _____
3. quality   _____
4. capacity   _____
5. charity   _____
6. city   _____
7. honesty   _____
8. equality   _____
9. necessity _____
10. university _____
11. priority   _____
12. variety   _____

Latin Shortcut

Here are the Latin words. Check if you got them right. You will also find many more words that you didn't know that you knew.

accessibilitas	curiositas	fraternitas
activitas	densitas	frugalitas
adversitas	difficultas	generalitas
affinitas	dignitas	generositas
agilitas	inaequalitas	hilaritas
ambiguitas	diversitas,	honestas
amoenitas	divinitas	hospitalitas
animositas	dualitas	hostilitas
anxietas	duplicitas	humanitas
annuitas	entitas	humiditas
atrocitas	aequitas	humilitas
auctoritas	specialitas	identitas
brevitas	spiritualitas	aequalitas
immanitas	stabilitas	impossibilitas
calamitas	sterilitas	improbabilitas
qualitas	aeternitas	impunitas
quantitas	facultas	incapacitas
capacitas	familiaritas	indignitas
caritas	fatalitas	individualitas
celebritas	feminitas	infallibilitas
civitas	ferocitas	inferioritas
civilitas	fecunditas	infidelitas
communitas	fidelitas	informalitas
continuitas	finalitas	immensitas
credibilitas	formalitas	immortalitas
crudelitas	fragilitatis	immunitas

Latin Shortcut

insecuritas
integritas
irregularitas
fidelitas
legalitas
libertas
longaevitas
magnanimitas
malleabilitas
mediocritas
modalitas
monstrositas
moralitas
mortalitas
necessitas
neutralitas
novitas
obesitas

obscoenitas
novitas
obscuritas
paritas
particularitas
paternitas
perpetuitas
personalitas
perversitas
pluralitas
possibilitas
posteritas
prioritas
probabilitas
proprietas
prosperitas
proximitas
realitas

sensibilitas
sensualitas
serenitas
simplicitas
singularitas
sobrietas
societas
trinitas
unitas
uniformitas
universitas
vanitas
varietas
virginitas
viscositas
viscositas
vitalitas

Latin Shortcut

CAPITULUM VI.
TOR

Words ending in **TOR** in English are exactly like the Latin ones with a few small spelling changes.

accelerator
accumulator
activator
actor
actuator
administrator
adulterator
aemulator
aequator
alternator
amalgamator
animator
annotator
anticipator
applicator
appretiator
appropriator
articulator
aspirator
assessor
assimilator
attenuator
auctor
auditor
authenticator
aviator
benefactor
calumniator
carburetor

circulator
clamor
cocreator
coinvestigator
collimator
color
commemorator
communicator
compactor
compositor
compressor
conciliator
condemnor
conductor
confessor
congratulator
congregator
consolidator
constructor
consultor
consummator
contaminator
contemplator
contradictor
cooperator
coordinator
coprocessor
corrector
correlator

creator
creditor
curator
debitor
decelerator
dedicator
defibrillator
defoliator
dehydrator
demodulator
demonstrator
denominator
depositor
desiccator
detector
determinator
detonator
deviator
dictator
dilator
director
discriminator
disintegrator
distributor
divisor
doctor
dolor
dominatior
duplicator

Latin Shortcut

editor
educator
elector
elevator
elutriator
emanator
emasculator
enumerator
enuntiator
eradicator
error
evaporator
expiator
expositor
expropriator
extensor
exterior
exterminator
extinctor
extirpator
extrapolator
fabulator
facilitator
factor
fascinator
fervor
flocculator
formulator
fractionator
fumigator
furor
generator
genitor
gesticulador
gladiator
graduator
granulator

gubernator
horror
humor
iaculator
illuminator
illustrator
imitator
immolator
impactor
imperator
implementor
impostor
improvisator
incinerator
incorporator
indicator
inferior
inflator
inflictor
initiator
inoculator
inquisitor
inseminator
inspector
instructor
insufflator
integrator
interceptor
intercessor
interdictor
interior
interlocutor
interoceptor
interpolator
interrogator
interruptor
intimidator

invalidator
inventor
inversor
irradiator
irrigator
legislator
liberator
liquor
lubricator
macerator
masticator
masturbator
matador
mediator
meditator
micromanipulator
microprocessor
migrator
minor
moderator
modulator
monochromator
mutilator
nada
narrator
negator
negotiator
nitrator
nomenclator
nominator
nucleator
numerator
obsessor
obstructor
operator
orator
orchestrator

Latin Shortcut

oscillator
oxygenator
pastor
percolator
perforator
persecutor
pollinator
posterior
postulator
Praedestinator
praeparator
praevaricator
predictor
preprocessor
procrastinator
procreator
professor
progenitor
pronator
propagator

propitiator
protector
radiator
reactor
redactor
relator
renovator
resonator
respirator
salvator
saturator
senator
senior
separator
simulator
speculator
splendor
stipulator
stupor
superior

supervisor
tabulator
tenor
terminator
terror
tractor
traditor
transgressor
translator
tumor
turbogenerator
tutor
vaccinator
valor
venditor
ventilator
vibrator
vigor
violator

Latin Shortcut

CAPITULUM VII.
ICUS

Words ending in **IC** or **ICAL** in English become **ICUS** in Latin.

Translate these words into Latin and then check the answers on the next page.

1. biological   _____
2. cynic   _____
3. classical   _____
4. economic   _____
5. electric   _____
6. magic   _____
7. mechanic   _____
8. poetic   _____
9. practical   _____
10. toxic   _____
11. traumatic   _____
12. typical   _____

Latin Shortcut

Here are the Latin words. Check if you got them right. You will also find many more words that you didn't know that you knew.

allergicus	epilepticus	metaphoricus
abecedarius	scepticus	methodicus
astronomicus	sphaericus	mysticus
biologicus	evangelicus	mythologicus
botanicus	fanaticus	numericus
cyclicus	pharmaceuticus	opticus
cylindrus	philosophicus	poeticus
cynicus	gastricus	politicus
classicus	geographicus	practicus
clinicus	geometricus	rhetoricus
colicus	hystericus	sabbaticus
comicus	historicus	satiricus
criticus	identicus	symmetrus
chronicus	ironicus	symptomaticus
cubicus	lyricus	technicus
diabolicus	logicus	theologicus
ecclesiasticus	logisticus	therapeuticus
oeconomicus	magicus	typicus
electricus	mathematicus	toxicus
empiricus	mechanicus	traumaticus

Latin Shortcut

CAPITULUM VIII.
ANTEM

Words ending in **ANT** in English become **ANTEM** in Latin.

Translate these words into Latin and then check the answers on the next page.

1. constant   _____
2. consonant   _____
3. elephant   _____
4. giant   _____
5. infant   _____
6. immigrant   _____
7. important   _____
8. insignificant _____
9. occupant   _____
10. protestant _____
11. participant _____
12. vibrant   _____

Latin Shortcut

Here are the Latin words. Check if you got them right. You will also find many more words that you didn't know that you knew.

abundantem	gigantem	officiantem
ambulantem	ignorantem	participantem
applicantem	immigrantem	praedominantem
arrogantem	importantem	praeponderantem
consonantem	incessantem	precipitantem
constantem	infantem	protestantem
declarantem	informantem	quadrantem
distantem	inhabitantem	radiantem
dominantem	insignificantem	redundantem
elegantem	instantem	relevantem
elephantem	intolerantem	resonantem
emigrantem	irritantem	resultantem
exorbitantem	mercatantem	supplicantem
expectantem	migrantem	triumphantem
extravagantem	militantem	vacantem
fulminantem	mutantem	vibrantem
fumigatem	occupantem	

CAPITULUM IX.
ENTEM

Words ending in **ENT** in English become **ENTEM** in Latin.

Translate these words into Latin and then check the answers on the next page.

1. accident _____
2. agent _____
3. coherent _____
4. competent _____
5. continent _____
6. excellent _____
7. equivalent _____
8. frequent _____
9. impatient _____
10. intelligent _____
11. president _____
12. urgent _____

Latin Shortcut

Here are the Latin words. Check if you got them right. You will also find many more words that you didn't know that you knew.

accidentem	aequivalentem	intermittentem
adiacentem	evidentem	latentem
adolescentem	excellentem	negligentem
agentem	frequentem	omnipraesentem
antecedentem	impatientem	omniscientem
apparentem	impertinentem	patientem
clientem	imprudentem	permanentem
cohaerentem	incandescentem	pertinentem
competentem	incidentem	praesidentum
continentem	incompetentem	recentem
contingentem	inconsequentem	residentem
decentem	indecentem	reticentem
detergentem	indifferentem	serpentem
differentem	indulgentem	torrentem
diligentem	ingredientem	transparentem
dissidentem	inhaerentem	urgentem
divergentem	innocentem	vehementem
eloquentem	insolentem	vicepraesidentem
eminentem	intelligentem	

Latin Shortcut

CAPITULUM X.
ARE

Words ending in **ATE** in English become **ARE** in Latin.

Translate these words into Latin and then check the answers on the next page.

1. accelerate _____
2. administrate _____
3. celebrate _____
4. contaminate _____
5. coordinate _____
6. educate _____
7. elaborate _____
8. formulate _____
9. immigrate _____
10. irritate _____
11. navigate _____
12. rotate _____

Latin Shortcut

Here are the Latin words. Check if you got them right. You will also find many more words that you didn't know that you knew.

abbreviare	cooperari	speculari
accelerare	coordinare	aestimare
accumulare	corroborare	strangulare
administrare	creare	evacuare
affiliare	cultivare	evaporare
gitare	debilitare	exaggerare
aggravare	decapitare	exasperare
allegáre	decorare	excavare
alienare,	degenerare	exfoliare
amputare	delegare	exterminare
animáre	denigrare	fabricare
anticipare	denuntiare	fascinare
appretiare	depretiare	felicitare
articulare	designare	filtrare
assassinare	deteriorare	formulare
assimilare	devastare	fornicari
associare	differentiare	frustrate
authenticare	dilatare	fumigare, fumare
calculare	disseminare	generare
castigare	dislocare	gesticulari
castrare	domesticare	habituare
celebrare	dominari	haesitare
circulare	duplicare	humiliare
coagulare	educare	imitari
compensare	elaborare	implicare
complicare	eliminare	inaugurare
communicare,	emanare	incinerare
condensare	emancipare	incriminare
confiscare	emigrare	incubare
conjugare	concentrare	indicare
consecrare	intrare	initiare
consolidare	enumerare	imigrare
contaminare	enuntiare	inoculare
contemplare	aequivocare	insinuare

Latin Shortcut

integrare	negotiari	renovare
interrogare	nominare	repatriare
intimidare	palpare	reiterare
intoxicare	participare	revalidare
investigare	perforare	rotare
irradiare	perpetuare	saturare
irrigare	predominare	separare
irritare	praemeditari	syncopare
lacerare	procrastinare	situare
liberare	propagare	subordinare
liquidare	recuperare	resuscitare
lubricare	refrigerare	tolerare
operari	regenerare	delineare
masticare	regulare	terminare
meditari	regurgitare	validare
mutilare	rehabilitare	vegetare
navigare	relegare	ventilare
necessitare	remunerare	

CAPITULUM XI.
ARIUS

Words ending in **ARY** in English become **ARIUS** in Latin.

Translate these words into Latin and then check the answers on the next page.

1. adversary _____
2. anniversary _____
3. contrary _____
4. dictionary _____
5. disciplinary _____
6. honorary _____
7. imaginary _____
8. ordinary _____
9. temporary _____
10. veterinary _____
11. vocabulary _____
12. voluntary _____

Latin Shortcut

Here are the Latin words. Check if you got them right. You will also find many more words that you didn't know that you knew.

adversarius	honorarius	primarius
anniversarius	imaginarius	salarius
arbitrarius	intermedius	sanctuarium*
binarius	involuntarius	secretarius
contrarius	legendarius	secundarius
coronarius	literarius	solitarius
culinarius	mercenarius	temporarius
dictionarius	monetarius	tertiarius
disciplinarius	necessarius	ternarius
dispensarius	notarius	veterinarius
stationarius	ordinarius	vocabularius
extraordinarius	ovarius	voluntarius
glossarium*	paenitentiarius	
hereditarius	planetarius	

Latin Shortcut

CAPITULUM XII.
MEMTUM

Words ending in **MENT** in English become **MEMTUM** in Latin.

Translate these words into Latin and then check the answers on the next page.

1. argument _____
2. armament _____
3. document _____
4. element _____
5. fundament _____
6. increment _____
7. instrument _____
8. medicament _____
9. monument _____
10. movement _____
11. parliament _____
12. sacrament _____

Latin Shortcut

Here are the Latin words. Check if you got them right. You will also find many more words that you didn't know that you knew.

ambientem*	firmamentum	parliamentum
argumentum	fragmentum	pigmentum
armamentum	fundamentum	regimentum
caementum	incrementum	rudimentum
complementum	instrumentum	sacramentum
condimentum	ligamentum	segmentum
decrementum	lineamentum	sentimentum
documentum	medicamentum	supplementum
elementum	monumentum	temperamentum
fermentum	movimentum	testamentum
filamentum	ornamentum	tormentum

Latin Shortcut

CAPITULUM XIII.
ENTIA

Words ending in **ENCE** in English become **ENTIA** in Latin.

Translate these words into Latin and then check the answers on the next page.

1. absence   _____
2. appearance   _____
3. circumference _____
4. correspondence _____
5. existence   _____
6. experience   _____
7. influence   _____
8. innocence   _____
9. intelligence   _____
10. license   _____
11. science   _____
12. violence   _____

Latin Shortcut

Here are the Latin words. Check if you got them right. You will also find many more words that you didn't know that you knew.

absentia
abstinentia
dhaerentia
adolescentia
antecedentia
cadentia
circumferentia
correspondentia
coincidentia
competentia
concupiscentia
conferentia
confluentia
congruentia
conscientia
consequentia
continentia
contingentia
convalescentia
corpulentia
influentia
violentia
decadentia
dehiscentia
differentia
diligentia
dissidentia
divergentia
effervescentia
effluentia
eloquentia
apparentia
eminentia
aequivalentia

essentia
evidentia
excellentia
exigentia
existentia
experientia
florentia
frequentia
imminentia
impatientia
impaenitentia
impertinentia
imprudentia
impudentia
incidentia
incongruentia
inconsequentia
incontinentia
indifferentia
indigentia
indolentia
indulgentia
inexistentia
inexperientia
inferentia
infrequentia
inhaerentia
innocentia
insolentia
intellegentia
irreverentia
iurisprudentia
licentia
magnificentia

munificentia
neglegentia
occurrentia
omnipraesentia
omniscientia
opulentia
patientia
paenitentia
permanentia
potentia
praeeminentia
praexistentia
preferentia
praescientia
praesentia
providentia
prudentia
pubescentia
quintaessentia
referentia
reminiscentia
residentia
scientia
sequentia
somnolentia
subsistentia
teleconferentia
tendentia
transparentia
turbulentia
valentia
videoconferentia
virulentia

CAPITULUM XIV.
BILIS

Words ending in **BLE** in English become **BILIS** in Latin.

Translate these words into Latin and then check the answers on the next page.

1. adorable   _____
2. calculable   _____
3. combustible   _____
4. comparable   _____
5. divisible   _____
6. favourable   _____
7. flexible   _____
8. honourable   _____
9. inevitable   _____
10. inexplicable   _____
11. possible   _____
12. probable   _____

Latin Shortcut

Here are the Latin words. Check if you got them right. You will also find many more words that you didn't know that you knew.

admirabilis
admissibilis
adorabilis
appretiabilis
audibilis
combustibilis
comparabilis
compatibilis
computabilis
considerabilis
consolabilis
consumptibilis
convertibilis
corruptibilis
culpabilis
demonstrabilis
deplorabilis
determinabilis
detestabilis
divisibilis
excitabilis
explicabilis
fallibilis
favorabilis
flexibilis
formidabilis
habitabilis
honorabilis

horribilis
imaginabilis
impeccabilis
impossibilis
improbabilis
inacceptabilis
inaccessibilis
inadmissibilis
inaestimabilis
inaudibilis
incomparabilis
incomprehensibilis
inconsolabilis
incorruptibilis
incurabilis
indispensabilis
indisputabilis
inevitabilis
inexplicabilis
infallibilis
inflammabilis
inflexibilis
insatiabilis
inseparabilis
insociabilis
intolerabilis
invariabilis
invisibilis

irreconcilabilis
irresistibilis
irrevocabilis
irritabilis
lamentabilis
legibilis
malleabilis
memorabilis
mercabilis
moderabilis
notabilis
observabilis
operabilis
palpabilis
plausibilis
possibilis
probabilis
reparabilis
responsabilis
separabilis
sociabilis
tangibilis
terribilis
tolerabilis
variabilis
visibilis
vulnerabilis

Latin Shortcut

CAPITULUM XV.
IVUS

Words ending in **IVE** in English become **IVUS** in Latin.

Translate these words into Latin and then check the answers on the next page.

1. active _____
2. adjective _____
3. communicative _____
4. comparative _____
5. decisive _____
6. digestive _____
7. excessive _____
8. exclusive _____
9. fugitive _____
10. imaginative _____
11. informative _____
12. intensive _____

Latin Shortcut

Here are the Latin words. Check if you got them right. You will also find many more words that you didn't know that you knew.

abortivus
ablativus
abusivus
accusativus
activus
adjectivus
administrativus
adoptivus
affectivus
appellativus
augmentativus
captivus
cognitivus
collectivus
communicativus
comparativus
compulsivus
concessivus
consecutivus
constitutivus
constructivus
contemplativus
continuativus
convulsivus
copulativus
correctivus
correlativus
corrosivus
curativus
dativus
decisivus
declarativus
deductivus
definitivus
demonstrativus
denominatus
descriptivus
destructivus
digestivus

diminutivus
discursivus
disintegrativus
disjunctivus
distinctivus
distributivus
electivus
excessivus
exclusivus
executivus
explicativus
expressivus
figurativus
foederatus*
frequentativus
fugitivus
generativus
genitivus
illativus
imaginativus
imitativus
imperativus
impulsivus
incisivus
indicativus
inductivus
infinitivus
informativus
intensivus
interrogativus
intransitivus
intuitivus
inventivus
lucrativus
motivus
multiplicativus
negativus
nominativus
nutritivus

objectivus
oppressivus
optativus
palliativus
partitivus
passivus
perfectivus
permissivus
persuasivus
positivus
possessivus
praedicativus
praescriptivus
primitivus
productivus
progressivus
prohibitivus
punitivus
putativus
qualitativus
quantitativus
receptivus
refractivus
relativus
repulsivus
respectivus
restrictivus
sedativus
speculativus
subiectivus
subjunctivus
substantivus
subversivus
successivus
superlativus
transitivus
vegetativus
vocativus
votivus

Latin Shortcut

CAPITULUM XVI.
FICARE

Words ending in **FY** in English become **FICARE** in Latin.

Translate these words into Latin and then check the answers on the next page.

1. amplify _____
2. certify _____
3. clarify _____
4. edify _____
5. identify _____
6. justify _____
7. modify _____
8. qualify _____
9. quantify _____
10. sanctify _____
11. scarify _____
12. simplify _____

Latin Shortcut

Here are the Latin words. Check if you got them right. You will also find many more words that you didn't know that you knew.

aedificare	pacificare
amplificare	petrificare
beatificar	purificare
certificare	qualificare
clarificare	quantificare
crucificare	ratificare
deificare	rectificare
diversificare	revivificare
exemplificare	sanctificare
falsificare	scarificare
fortificare	simplificare
fructificare	specificare
glorificare	stratificare
identificare	unificare
justificare	verificare
modificare	vivificare
mortificare	

Latin Shortcut

CAPITULUM XVII.
GIA

Words ending in **GY** in English become **GIA** in Latin.

Translate these words into Latin and then check the answers on the next page.

1. mythology _____
2. neurology _____
3. ornithology _____
4. osteology _____
5. pharmacology _____
6. philology _____
7. phraseology _____
8. physiology _____
9. psychology _____
10. strategy _____
11. synergy _____
12. trilogy _____

Latin Shortcut

Here are the Latin words. Check if you got them right. You will also find many more words that you didn't know that you knew.

trilogia	phraseologia
muthologia	physiologia
neurologia	polyphagia
omophagia	psychologia
ontologia	strategia
orgia	synergia
ornithologia	taumaturgia
osteologia	tautologia
paedagogia	theologia
pharmacologia	urologia
philologia	zoologia

Latin Shortcut

CAPITULUM XVIII.
ORIUS

Words ending in **ORY** in English become **ORIUS** in Latin.

Translate these words into Latin and then check the answers on the next page.

1. accusatory _____
2. conservatory _____
3. contradictory _____
4. interlocutory _____
5. laboratory _____
6. obligatory _____
7. observatory _____
8. oratory _____
9. peremptory _____
10. purgatory _____
11. repertory _____
12. respiratory _____

Latin Shortcut

Here are the Latin words. Check if you got them right. You will also find many more words that you didn't know that you knew.

accessorius

accusatorius

conservatorius

contradictorius

diffamatorius

exploratorius

gloria*

historia*

interlocutorius

laboratorius

memoria*

obligatorius

observatorius

oratorius

peremptorius

praeparatorius

purgatorius

repertorius

respiratorius

suppositorius

territorium*

trajectorius

victoria*

Latin Shortcut

CAPITULUM XIX.
IDUS

Words ending in **ID** in English become **IDUS** in Latin.

Translate these words into English.

1. acidus _____
2. aridus _____
3. avidus _____
4. bifidus _____
5. candidus _____
6. fluidus _____
7. frigidus _____
8. humidus _____
9. insipidus _____
10. invalidus _____
11. limpidus _____
12. liquidus _____
13. lividus _____
14. lucidus _____
15. morbidus _____
16. rigidus _____

CAPITULUM XX.
IZARE

Words ending in **IZE** in English become **IZARE** in Latin.

Translate these words into Latin and then check the answers on the next page.

1. analyze _____
2. authorize _____
3. baptize _____
4. characterize _____
5. evangelize _____
6. exorcize _____
7. fraternize _____
8. improvise _____
9. moralize _____
10. organize _____
11. prophetize _____
12. symbolize _____

Latin Shortcut

Here are the Latin words. Check if you got them right. You will also find many more words that you didn't know that you knew

analysare

actualizare

alcalinizare

almacenare

auctorizare

baptizare

characterizare

evangelizare

exorcizare

fraternizare

improvisare

moralizare

organizare

prophetizare

scandalizare

symbolizare

Latin Shortcut

CAPITULUM XXI.
ANTIA

Words ending in **ANCE** in English become **ANTIA** in Latin.

Translate these words into Latin and then check the answers on the next page.

1. ambulance   _____
2. arrogance   _____
3. circumstance   _____
4. concordance   _____
5. distance   _____
6. extravagance   _____
7. flagrance   _____
8. ignorance   _____
9. importance   _____
10. perseverance   _____
11. substance   _____
12. tolerance   _____

Latin Shortcut

Here are the Latin words. Check if you got them right. You will also find many more words that you didn't know that you knew.

abundantia	flagrantia	praeponderantia
ambulantia	ignorantia	protuberantia
arrogantia	importantia	repugnantia
circumstantia	insignificantia	resonantia
concordantia	intemperantia	substantia
consonantia	intolerantia	tolerantia
dissonantia	irradiantia	vigilantia
distantia	luminantia	
extravagantia	perseverantia	

Latin Shortcut

CAPITULUM XXII.
OSUS

Words ending in **OUS** in English become **OSUS** in Latin.

Translate these words into Latin and then check the answers on the next page.

1. ambitious   _____
2. religious   _____
3. victorious _____
4. vicious   _____
5. industrious _____
6. ingenious   _____
7. spacious   _____
8. studious   _____
9. fabulous   _____
10. furious   _____
11. delicious _____
12. precious   _____

Latin Shortcut

Here are the Latin words. Check if you got them right. You will also find many more words that you didn't know that you knew.

aluminosus	ingeniosus	religiosus
ambitiosus	insidiosus	rigorosus
amorosus	invidiosus	ruinosus
anxius	laboriosus	scabrosus
biliosus	leprosus	scandalosus
bulbosus	libidinosus	scrophulosus
caerimoniosus	licentiosus	scrupulosus
calamitosus	litigiosus	seditiosus
captiosus	luminosus	sententiosus
cavernosus	luxuriosus	serosus
compendiosus	malitiosus	sinuosus
contagiosus	miraculosus	spatiosus
copiosus	monstrosus	speciosus
curiosus	montaneosus	studiosus
deliciosus	mucosus	superstitiosus
fabulosus	muscilaginosus	taediosus
factiosus	nebulosus	tenebrosus
fastidiosus	nervosus	tortuosus
fibrosus	nitrosus	tumultuosus
furiosus	numerosus	vertiginosus
generosus	odiosus	victoriosus
gloriosus	perniciosus	vinosus
glutinosus	pomposus	virtuosus
gratiosus	porosus	viscosus
ignominiosus	praestigiosus	vitiosus
incestuosus	praesumptuosus	voluminosus
incuriosus	pretiosus	
industriosus	prodigiosus	

Latin Shortcut

CAPITULUM XXIII.
SIS

Most English words that end in **SIS** are exactly like the Latin ones with a few small spelling changes.

amaurosis	chromatolysis	osmosis
analysis	dialysis	osteoporosis
ankylosis	fibrosis	otosclerosis
anthesis	genesis	ovogenesis
antibiosis	gnosis	paedomorphosis
antiphrasis	haemodialysis	parentesis
antithesis	hypnosis	partenogenesis
aphairesis	hypostasis	pedogenesis
apotheosis	hypothesis	petrogenesis
arteriosclerosis	katalusis	photosynthesis
arthrodesis	katekhesis	pinocitosis
atherosclerosis	kirrhosis	pirolisis
babesiosis	krisis	plasmaferesis
bacteriostasis	leptospirosis	poliedrosis
biocenosis	metamorphosis	poligenesis
byssinosis	mycosis	polinosis
catachresis	neurosis	prosthesis

Latin Shortcut

- protasis
- proteolisis
- protesis
- psicogenesis
- psiconeurosis
- psicosintesis
- psitacosis
- psykhosis
- quimiosintesis
- radiolysis
- reanalisis
- resintesis
- salmonelosis
- sarcoidosis
- sarcomatosis
- siderosis
- silepsis
- silicosis
- simbiosis
- sindesmosis
- sineresis
- sinfisis
- sinostosis
- solvolisis
- synthesis
- teniasis
- thesis
- thrombosis
- tirotoxicosis
- toxicosis
- toxoplasmosis
- tricomoniasis
- tripanosomiasis
- triquinosis
- tuberculosis
- tumorigenesis
- urolitiasis
- virosis
- vitelogenesis
- xerosis
- zoonosis

Latin Shortcut

CAPITULUM XXIV.
ISMUS

Words ending in **ISM** in English become **ISMUS** in Latin.

Translate these words into Latin and then check the answers on the next page.

1. alcoholism _____
2. atheism _____
3. autism _____
4. baptism _____
5. capitalism _____
6. evangelism _____
7. pessimism _____
8. racism _____
9. socialism _____
10. spiritualism _____
11. symbolism _____
12. vandalism _____

Latin Shortcut

Here are the Latin words. Check if you got them right. You will also find many more words that you didn't know that you knew.

absenteeismus	contraterrorismus	puritanismus
alcoholismus	euphemismus	racismus
anarchismus	evangelismus	sexismus
anticapitalismus	exorcismus	socialismus
antifascismus	feminismus	spiritualismus
atheismus	fundamentorismus	surrealismus
autismus	mechanismus	symbolismus
baptismus	metabolismus	truismus
Buddhismus	pessimismus	vandalismus
Capitalismus	pragmatismus	vegetarianismus
conservatismus	protectionismus	

Latin Shortcut

CAPITULUM XXV.
GRAMMA

Words ending in **GRAM** in English become **GRAMMA** in Latin.

Translate these words into Latin and then check the answers on the next page.

1. aerogram _____
2. cardiogram _____
3. centigram _____
4. decigram _____
5. diagram _____
6. electrogram _____
7. gram _____
8. hologram _____
9. ideogram _____
10. kilogram _____
11. radiogram _____
12. telegram _____

Latin Shortcut

Here are the Latin words. Check if you got them right. You will also find many more words that you didn't know that you knew.

aerogramma	gramma
anagramma	hexagramma
audiogramma	histogramma
autoradiogramma	hologramma
barogramma	ideogramma
cablegramma	kilogramma
cardiogramma	microgramma
centigramma	milligramma
cladogramma	monogramma
cryptogramma	nomogramma
decigramma	oscillogramma
dekagrammaa	parallelogrammum
dendrogramma	phanerogama
diogramma	phonogramma
echocardiogramma	photogramma
echogramma	pictogramma
electrogramma	radiogramma
electromyogramma	seismogramma
electropherogramma	spectrogramma
engramma	stereogramma
epigramma	telegramma

Latin Shortcut

CAPITULUM XXVI.
EMA

Words ending in **EM** in English become **EMA** in Latin.

Translate these words into Latin and then check the answers on the next page.

1. esteem _____
2. ecosystem _____
3. emblem _____
4. gem _____
5. photosystem _____
6. poem _____
7. problem _____
8. protoxylem _____
9. stratagem _____
10. subsystem _____
11. system _____
12. theorem _____

Latin Shortcut

Here are the Latin words. Check if you got them right. You will also find many more words that you didn't know that you knew.

aestima	protoxylema
ecosystema	stratagema
emblema	subproblema
exanthema	subsystema
gemma	supersystema
photosystema	systema
poema	theorema
problema	xylema
protophloema	

Latin Shortcut

CAPITULUM XXVII.
UM

Most English words that end in **UM** are exactly like the Latin ones with a few small spelling changes.

aecium
aequilibrium
album
aluminium
apothecium
aquarium
arboretum
argumentum
auditorium
aurum
calcium
coliseum
condominium
continuum
cranium
cubiculum
dominium
electrum
exemplum
forum
gymnasium
helium
hospilium
ieiunum
imperium
indicium

latifundium
lithium
magisterium
magnesium
magnum
maximum
mediterraneum
medium
memorandum
millennium
minimum
momentum
monochasium
museum
odium
optimum
origanum
ovum
palladium
parapodium
patagium
pendulum
Penicillium
petroleum
philtrum
phosphonium

planetarium
podium
potassium
praesidium
premium
principium
quorum
radium
referendum
rosarium
sanatorium
sanctum
sanitarium
secundum
sensorium
sensum
sodium
stadium
timpanum
titanium
ultimatum
uranium
vacuum
vestigium

Latin Shortcut

CAPITULUM XXVIII.
URA

Words ending in **URE** in English become **URA** in Latin.

Translate these words into Latin and then check the answers on the next page.

1. adventure _____
2. agriculture _____
3. armature _____
4. creature _____
5. culture _____
6. literature _____
7. scripture _____
8. stature _____
9. structure _____
10. temperature _____
11. texture _____
12. torture _____

Latin Shortcut

Here are the Latin words. Check if you got them right. You will also find many more words that you didn't know that you knew.

acupunctura
adventura
agricultura
apertura
apicultura
arboricultura
architectura
armatura
avicultura
candidatura
caricatura
censura
conjetura
contextura
creatura
cultura
curvatura
fissura
flexura

floricultura
fractura
genitura
horticultura
impostura
incisura
infraestructura
investitura
judicatura
legislatura
ligatura
litteratura
macroestructura
magistratura
miniatura
musculatura
nomenclatura
piscicultura
porphura

positura
primogenitura
ruptura
scriptura
sculptura
sepultura
statura
structura
subcultura
subliteratura
subminiatura
superestructura
tablatura
temperatura
textura
tortura
vasculatura
vestitura

Latin Shortcut

CAPITULUM XXIX.
TUDO

Words ending in **TUDE** in English become **TUDO** in Latin.

Translate these words into Latin and then check the answers on the next page.

1. altitude   _____

2. amplitude   _____

3. aptitude   _____

4. gratitude   _____

5. habitude   _____

6. latitude   _____

7. longitude   _____

8. magnitude   _____

9. multitude   _____

10. plenitude   _____

11. similitude   _____

Latin Shortcut

Here are the Latin words. Check if you got them right. You will also find many more words that you didn't know that you knew.

altitudo	latitudo
amplitudo	longitudo
aptitudo	magnitudo
dissimilitudo	multitudo
exactitudo	negritudo
gratitudo	plenitudo
habitudo	prontitudo
ineptitudo	quietudo
inexactitudo	rectitudo
infinitudo	similitudo
ingratitudo	sollicitudo
inquietudo	vicissitudo

Latin Shortcut

CAPITULUM XXX.
TIA

Words ending in **CY** in English become **TIA** in Latin.

Translate these words into Latin and then check the answers on the next page.

1. agency _____
2. aristocracy _____
3. bureaucracy _____
4. emergency _____
5. pharmacy _____
6. frequency _____
7. presidency _____
8. sufficiency _____
9. diplomacy _____
10. chiromancy _____
11. tendency _____
12. infancy _____

Latin Shortcut

Here are the Latin words. Check if you got them right. You will also find many more words that you didn't know that you knew.

absorbentia	diplomatia	innocentia
aequivalentia	discordantia	insignificantia
agentia	discrepantia	insistentia
apetentia	divergentia	insufficientia
aristocratia	efficientia	insolventia
astringentia	elegantia	interdependentia
autocratia	emergentia	intermittentia
bureaucratia	eminentia	irrelevantia
cadentia	excellentia	meritocratia
chiromantia	exigentia	militantia
clementia	extravagantia	pendentia
cohaerentia	exuberantia	permanentia
competentia	flagrantia	persistentia
complacentia	fragantia	pharmatia
concurrentia	frequentia	potentia
congruentia	imminentia	presidentia
consistentia	impotentia	prominentia
constantia	inclementia	redundantia
contingentia	incompetentia	residentia
convenientia	inconsequentia	resistentia
corpulentia	inconstantia	sufficientia
decadentia	incontinentia	tendentia
decentia	indecentia	transparentia
deficientia	independentia	turbulentia
delinquentia	indifferentia	urgentia
democratia	inefficientia	valentia
dependentia	infantia	
detergentia	infrequentia	

Latin Shortcut

CAPITULUM XXXI.
PHIA

Words ending in **PHY** in English become **PHIA** in Latin.

Translate these words into Latin and then check the answers on the next page.

1. atrophy _____

2. autobiography _____

3. autography _____

4. bibliography _____

5. biography _____

6. discography _____

7. geography _____

8. calligraphy _____

9. orthography _____

10. philosophy _____

11. photography _____

12. radiography _____

Latin Shortcut

Here are the Latin words. Check if you got them right. You will also find many more words that you didn't know that you knew.

atrophia	discographia	radiographia
autobiographia	ecographia	sophia
autographia	geographia	telegraphia
bibliographia	historiographia	thermographia
biographia	kalligraphia	topographia
cacographia	orthographia	typographia
cartographia	philosophia	videographia
ceanographia	photographia	
choreographia	pornographia	

Latin Shortcut

CAPITULUM XXXII.
ESSUS

Words ending in **ESS** in English become **ESSUS** in Latin.

Translate these words into English.

1. abscessus _____
2. accessus _____
3. congressus _____
4. egressus _____
5. excessus _____
6. expressus _____
7. ingressus _____
8. obsessus _____
9. processus _____
10. progressus _____
11. confessus _____

CAPITULUM XXXIII.
GUS

Words ending in **GUE** in English become **GUS** in Latin.

Translate these words into English.

1. apologue   _____

2. catalogue   _____

3. decalogue   _____

4. dialogue   _____

5. epilogue   _____

6. homologue   _____

7. monologue   _____

8. pedagogue   _____

CAPITULUM XXXIV.
EA

Most English words that end in **EA** are exactly like the Latin ones with a few small spelling changes.

area	idea
azalea	miscellanea
centaurea	nausea
Corea	olea
cornea	palea
diarrhoea	panacea
dulcinea	seborrhoea
fovea	trachea
gonorrhoia	trochlea
guinea	urea
helodea	uvea

Latin Shortcut

CAPITULUM XXXV.
CULUM

Words ending in **CLE** in English become **CULUM** in Latin.

Translate these words into Latin and then check the answers on the next page.

1. testicle _____
2. article _____
3. circle _____
4. fascicle _____
5. monocle _____
6. muscle _____
7. obstacle _____
8. oracle _____
9. pentacle _____
10. spectacle _____
11. tabernacle _____
12. vehicle _____

Latin Shortcut

Here are the Latin words. Check if you got them right. You will also find many more words that you didn't know that you knew.

tentaculum	epicyclum	ossiculum
testiculum	fasciculum	pediculum
articulum	folliculum	pedunculum
circulum	funiculum	pentaculum
coenaculum	furunculum	pinnaculum
corpusculum	monoculum	spectaculum
cubiculum	musculus	spiraculum
cyclum	obstaculum	tabernaculum
denticulum	oraculum	vehiculum

Latin Shortcut

CAPITULUM XXXVI.
US

Words ending in **AN** in English become Latin by adding **US** at the end of them.

Translate these words into Latin and then check the answers on the next page.

1. christian _____

2. human _____

3. ocean _____

4. organ _____

5. pagan _____

6. republican _____

7. roman _____

8. samaritan _____

9. spartan _____

10. urban _____

11. vegetarian _____

12. vulcan _____

Latin Shortcut

Here are the Latin words. Check if you got them right. You will also find many more words that you didn't know that you knew.

antichristianus	paganus
antihumanus	publicanus
christianus	quotidianus
cyprianus	republicanus
decanus	romanus
diocesanus	samaritanus
humanus	spartanus
interurbanus	urbanus
meridianus	vegetarianus
metropolitanus	veteranus
oceanus	vulcanus
organus	

Latin Shortcut

CAPITULUM XXXVII.
IA

Most English words that end in **IA** are exactly like the Latin ones with a few small spelling changes.

atrophia	diphtheria
academia	dyslexia
acrophobia	encyclopaedia
amnesia	euphoria
anaimia	euthanasia
anaisthesia	gloria
analgesia	hernia
anorexia	homophobia
asphyxia	hyperthermia
bacteria	Phobia
bohemia	

CAPITULUM XXXVIII.
PLUM or PLUS

Words ending in **PLE** in English become **PLUM** in the **Singular** and or **PLUS** in the Plural in Latin.

Translate these words into English:

1. amplum _____
2. entuplum _____
3. discipulum _____
4. exemplum _____
5. participium _____
6. principium _____
7. quadruplum _____
8. scrupulum _____
9. sextuplum _____
10. simplum _____
11. submultiplus _____
12. templum _____

CAPITULUM XXXIX. ARIS

Words ending in **AR** in English become **ARIS** in in Latin.

Translate these words into Latin and then check the answers on the next page.

1. angular _____
2. circular _____
3. curricular _____
4. familiar _____
5. irregular _____
6. particular _____
7. peculiar _____
8. popular _____
9. rectangular _____
10. similar _____
11. solar _____
12. triangular _____

Latin Shortcut

altaris	consularis	polaris
angularis	curricularis	popularis
annularis	exemplaris	quadrangularis
antinuclearis	familiaris	rectangularis
antipopularis	impopularis	regularis
antisolaris	irregularis	similaris
apendicularis	lunaris	singularis
articularis	modularis	solaris
avicularis	molecularis	tabularis
baris	muscularis	testicularis
bimolecularis	nuclearis	triangularis
binocularis	ocularis	unicellularis
bipolaris	particularis	vascularis
cardiovascularis	peculiaris	
cellularis	perpendicularis	
circularis	pilaris	

Latin Shortcut

CAPITULUM XL.
TRUM

Words ending in **TER** in English become **TRUM** in Latin.

Translate these words into Latin and then check the answers on the next page.

1. centimeter _____
2. center _____
3. chronometer _____
4. filter _____
5. liter _____
6. meter _____
7. minister _____
8. monster _____
9. neuter _____
10. parameter _____
11. register _____
12. thermometer _____

Latin Shortcut

Here are the Latin words. Check if you got them right. You will also find many more words that you didn't know that you knew.

accelerometrum	electrometrum	perimetum
arbitrum	filtrum	presbyterum
capitulum	Helicopterum	registrum
carpentum	litrum	spectrum
centimetrum	magistrum	subcentrum
centrum	metrum	taximetrum
cetrum	ministrum	theatrum
chiliometrum	monstrum	thermometrum
chronometrum	neutrum	velocimetrum
diametrum	parametrum	

CAPITULUM XLI.
ETUM

Words ending in **ET** in English become **ETUM** in Latin.

Translate these words into English.

1. alphabetum   _____
2. amuletum   _____
3. apparatum   _____
4. discretum   _____
5. indiscretum   _____
6. magnetum   _____
7. secretum   _____
8. sonnetum   _____

Latin Shortcut

CAPITULUM XLII.
ENSUS

Words ending in **ENSE** in English become **ENSUS** in Latin.

Translate these words into English.

1. densus _____

2. incensus _____

3. immensus _____

4. intensus _____

5. offensus _____

6. tensus _____

7. ultradensus _____

8. defensus _____

9. propensus _____

CAPITULUM XLIII.
Numeri Romani

1: I
2: II
3: III
4: IV
5: V
6: VI
7: VII
8: VIII
9: IX
10: X
11: XI
12: XII
13: XIII
14: XIV
15: XV
16: XVI
17: XVII
18: XVIII
19: XIX
20: XX
21: XXI
22: XXII
23: XXIII
24: XXIV
25: XXV
26: XXVI
27: XXVII
28: XXVIII
29: XXIX
30: XXX
31: XXXI
32: XXXII
33: XXXIII
34: XXXIV
35: XXXV
36: XXXVI
37: XXXVII
38: XXXVIII
39: XXXIX
40: XL
41: XLI
42: XLII
43: XLIII
44: XLIV
45: XLV
46: XLVI
47: XLVII
48: XLVIII
49: XLIX
50: L
51: LI
52: LII
53: LIII
54: LIV
55: LV
56: LVI
57: LVII
58: LVIII
59: LIX
60: LX
61: LXI
62: LXII
63: LXIII
64: LXIV
65: LXV
66: LXVI
67: LXVII
68: LXVIII
69: LXIX
70: LXX
71: LXXI
72: LXXII
73: LXXIII
74: LXXIV
75: LXXV
76: LXXVI
77: LXXVII
78: LXXVIII
79: LXXIX
80: LXXX
81: LXXXI
82: LXXXII
83: LXXXIII
84: LXXXIV
85: LXXXV
86: LXXXVI
87: LXXXVII
88: LXXXVIII
89: LXXXIX
90: XC
91: XCI
92: XCII
93: XCIII
94: XCIV
95: XCV
96: XCVI
97: XCVII
98: XCVIII
99: XCIX
100: C
101: CI
500: D
1,000: M

Talk to the Author
Email: irineu@oliveiralanguageservices.com

Made in the USA
San Bernardino, CA
12 January 2018

Made in the USA
San Bernardino, CA
12 January 2018